LIFE OF THE KELP FOREST

UNDER THE SEA

Lynn M. Stone

Rourke Publishing LLC
Vero Beach, Florida 32964

www.rourkepublishing.com

PHOTO CREDITS:
All photographs ©Marty Snyderman except pgs 13, 17, 21 ©Lynn M. Stone

EDITORIAL SERVICES:
Pamela Schroeder

Library of Congress Cataloging-in-Publication Data

Stone, Lynn M.
    Life of the kelp forest / Lynn M. Stone.
        p. cm. — (Under the sea)
    Includes bibliographical references (p.24)
    ISBN 1-58952-112-9
    1. Kelp bed ecology—Juvenile literature. [1. Kelp bed ecology. 2. Kelps.
3. Marine animals. 4. Marine plants. 5. Ecology.] I. Title

QH541.5.K4 S76 2001
579.8'8717—dc21

                                                        2001019423

Printed in the USA

TABLE OF CONTENTS

THE KELP FOREST

Forests on the land are the homes of tall trees. A different kind of forest lies under the cold, rocky seas not far from some seashores.

These forests don't have trees. Instead, they are homes for giant **kelp** plants. Giant kelp is a type of brown seaweed. Giant kelp has a long center stalk, like a corn plant. Flat, ribbon-like leaves called "blades" branch from the stalk. The stalk attaches itself to rocks.

A diver swims among towering stalks of giant kelp.

Each blade of the stalk has an air-filled **bladder**. The kelp bladders look and act like little balloons. Each floating bladder helps lift the kelp stalk and blades up toward the ocean surface.

A giant kelp plant can rise over 100 feet (30 meters) and spread another 100 feet (30 m) on the ocean surface. Surface kelp forms a ceiling of kelp stalks and blades. Under the ceiling, the tall kelp plants make a leafy undersea forest.

Bladders lift kelp to the sea surface over a California kelp forest.

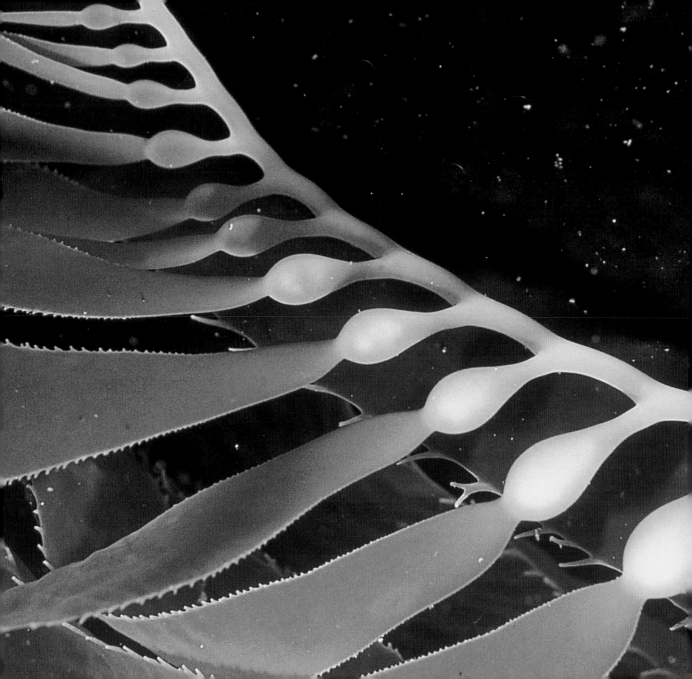

THE FOREST COMMUNITY

A forest of trees is a home for many **species**, or kinds, of animals. A kelp forest is, too. A kelp forest in southern California may have more than 800 kinds of fish and small animals. One kelp plant may have more than 1 million small animals on it!

The California sea lion is one of hundreds of kinds of marine animals that hunt in the kelp forest.

All these animals can weigh down kelp blades. The blades can't reach up to the sunlight. The kelp plant needs sunlight for food. So kelp plants shed their old blades often and quickly grow new ones. Giant kelp are among the world's fastest growing plants. Some of the largest kinds grow 2 feet (60 centimeters) in one day!

A bat ray cruises through a forest of giant kelp.

The copper rockfish of California kelp forests is also called the chuckle-head.

In healthy kelp forests, sea urchins feed mostly on decaying kelp before becoming prey for sea otters and people.

Kelp drop tons of old blades back into the sea. It is not wasted. The old, dead blades **decay**. Decaying kelp becomes food—and energy—for all kinds of tiny **marine** creatures. Some of these animals are too small to see. But they are very important food for animals we can see. The kelp itself is a major food for all animals of the community.

A diver in a kelp forest swims toward blacksmith fish, kelp bass, and senorita fish.

LITTLE ANIMALS

A kelp forest is home for many small, boneless animals called **invertebrates**. Some of the invertebrates, like the octopus, are among the best-known animals in the sea.

A well-known invertebrate of the California coast is the abalone. The abalone is a kind of snail. People like abalones for their meat and beautiful inner shells. Abalones feed on kelp. Sea urchins, kelp snails, lobsters, and soft, plump sea hares feed on kelp, too.

People prize abalone for its meat and the pearly finish of the inside of its shell.

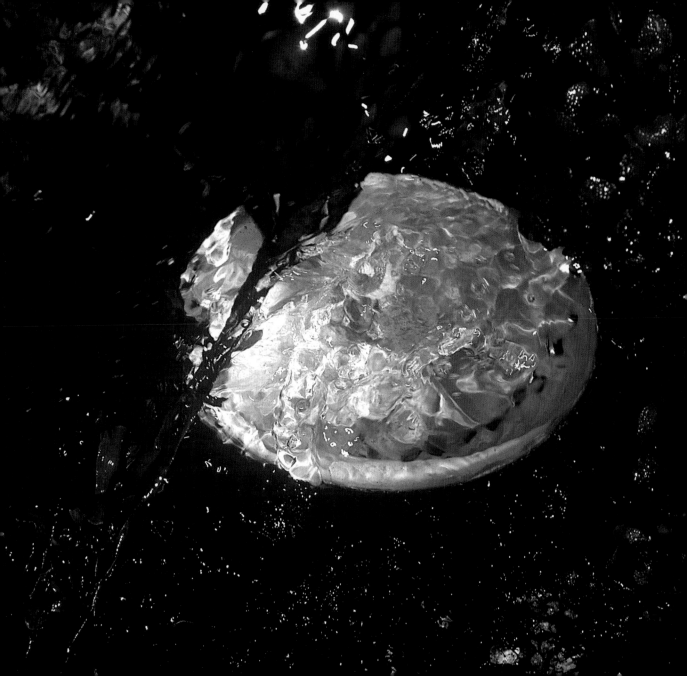

The kelp forest hides other invertebrates you may know. Some are sea-anemone, bat stars, corals, barnacles, sea cucumbers, and colorful sea slugs. Like sea hares, sea slugs are soft, snail-like animals without shells.

SEA OTTERS

Sea otters dive into the kelp to find urchins, abalones, and clams. A sea otter is one of the few animals to use "tools." The sea otter's tool is a rock that it grabs from the sea bottom. While swimming on its back, the sea otter holds the rock against its chest. An otter breaks open hard-shelled animals by smashing them against the rock.

After smashing open a clam, a sea otter enjoys a clam snack.

The bright orange garibaldi (see cover) is California's state marine fish. It lives in the kelp. More than 60 species of rockfish swim near the kelp forest bottom. Yellowtail, barracuda, sea bass, and sharks on the hunt pass through the kelp.

GLOSSARY

bladder (BLAD er) — an air-filled, balloon-like organ at the base of kelp blades

decay (di KAY) — to rot; how dead plants and animals are broken down into tiny particles

invertebrate (in VER teh brit) — any one of several groups of boneless and usually small animals, such as spiders, worms, snails, crabs, and starfish

kelp (KELP) — a type of seaweed; a brown marine algae

marine (meh REEN) — of the sea

species (SPEE sheez) — within a group of closely related animals, such as seals, one certain kind (*harbor* seal)

INDEX

Further Reading

Swanson, Diane. *Safari Beneath the Sea*. Sierra Club Books, 1996
Wu, Norbert. *Beneath the Waves: Exploring the Hidden World of the Kelp Forest.*
    Chronicle, 1997.

Websites To Visit

•www.nationalgeographic.com/monterey.com
•www.mbayaq.org/

About The Author

Lynn Stone is the author of over 400 children's books. He is a talented natural history photographer as well. Lynn, a former teacher, travels worldwide to photograph wildlife in their natural habitat.